Ride Collector

Maine to Mississippi in

Five Days,

Twenty-five Rides,

Four Dollars & Forty Cents

Wade C Davis

The events depicted in this story are real, though names
and descriptions may be changed to preserve the
anonymity of the individuals described, and to
accommodate the failing memory of the author.

Published with support from Double Pixel Publications.
www.doublepixelpublications.com

ISBN: 1-62083-008-6
ISBN-13: 978-1-62083-008-6

DEDICATION

This book is dedicated to my mom, who both
encouraged me to write this book and
railed against me for having done this in the first
place.

Sorry, I'll never do it again.

(But don't read my book about hitchhiking in
Australia in January & February of 1995,
if I ever write that one.)

CONTENTS

Prologue

I used to tell people I would die before I was 30, or live to be at least 82 – and I believe I went through more than my fair share of guardian angels on my way to my 30th birthday. Hitchhiking from Maine to Mississippi at the end of the summer of '93 was a perfect example. 5 days, 25 rides, $4.40. Sounds exciting, daring – maybe even sexy. But it wasn't. Well, certainly not sexy. (You try feeling sexy after sleeping on the side of the interstate for several nights, not showering – why did these people let me into their cars again? – and relying on the goodness of strangers and a ragged, tag-team band of angels trying to keep you alive.) Not really daring, either – stupid, perhaps, but not daring.

And while there was some level of excitement at times, the vast majority of a hitchhiker's time is spent on the side of a highway, alternating between hope and despair. Those seem to be far from each other when you contemplate them from the comfy chair in your living room, but they may as well be intertwined lovers when you've been standing in the blazing sun at an interstate on-ramp for over three hours looking for the brake lights that might replace the tedium of immobility with the tedium of riding in an unknown car for an unspecified distance on the vast, unchanging U.S. interstate system.

So why and how did I get myself into this 'adventure'? Well, it all started, as so many great adventures do, when I tried to pull an April Fool's prank in college. We were going to move a ten foot tall, twenty foot long metal insect sculpture from the library to the student union. We got caught in the act. Sadly for me, I was already on disciplinary probation for throwing a nude pool party the previous term. Happily for me, the Dean of Students liked me – at least enough to not follow the letter of the law and throw me out of school. Instead, he gave us all a dose of community service. I had to dust books in the library, which, in some odd way, made the punishment fit the crime.

When I came across the book *Vagabonding in Europe and North Africa*, I decided, both figuratively and literally, to check it out. I learned a few things about hitchhiking, and a seed was planted in my brain. It took a couple of months to bear fruit, but my friend Evan helped with that. He and I were cabin counselors together at a summer camp in Vermont. When the summer was over, he told me he was hitchhiking to Maine and invited me along. I'd taken a leave of absence from school (to give the dust some time to settle and allow my disciplinary probation to expire), so I decided to tag along.

Over the two days that it took us to reach Bar Harbor, Evan taught me some of the realities that the book had missed. I learned that older Volvos are more likely to offer rides than VW busses. (One such Volvo station wagon that stopped for me was filled with a huge slab of marble – the driver was a sculptor who showed me photo albums filled with pictures of his work at the Baha'i Temple in Haifa, Israel.) I learned that one person can get a ride easier than two. I learned that it's okay to turn down a ride if you get an icky feeling about a person or a car. (Okay, I was taught that lesson; day two and day three would prove that I didn't learn it that well.) And I learned that the single greatest asset I had for obtaining a ride while hitchhiking was my guitar. (Learned this one by letting Evan 'carry it for me.' Sly guy, that

Evan.)

We were separated early on the first day, me in one car, with Evan on the side of the road waiting for the next obliging soul to come along. I continued on my way, still trying to remember all Evan had told me. One such nugget of wisdom was that, while you might be able to travel further, faster by hitchhiking on the interstate, it was illegal to do so on the Maine Turnpike. Thus, after I'd crossed into Maine, I exited the interstate with the car that carried me across the river from Portsmouth, and sat on the side of US 1 for several hours as darkness fell. Keep in mind this was before the days of the ubiquitous cell phone, so I had little hope of finding Evan, and I decided to think about a place to sleep. I walked in to the wooded area at the edge of the road. About a dozen yards in, I came upon a fence that blocked access to the interstate from the side. Beyond the rest of the grove in front of me, I could make out the headlights of the cars passing on the Turnpike. I believe this was a seminal moment for me. On one hand, I was essentially homeless and alone, stuck on the side of the road, with little to no money; on the other hand, I've just come out of a summer sleeping in an open-aired cabin in the woods when I wasn't sleeping in a tent on the trail. What's so different about being near a road, except it's louder and the air's not quite as fresh? I relaxed and decided to string up my hammock between two trees and camp for the night. My mind remembers being calm and collected and content with the whole situation, though I've discovered in life that the mind tends to remember the positives in situations longer than the discomforts. So there may have been some gnashing of teeth, self-pity, or even tears. That may explain why, when I ran into Evan late the next morning when he convinced the car he was in to stop to pick me up, I felt such a strong envy for the way he had passed his night: sleeping on a couch next to a fireplace after having spent the evening drinking beer with another of our camp friends who'd picked him up in New Hampshire and driven him to her house in Maine. We had to split up again after that ride, but I found that my self-confidence had increased. Here I was, the newbie to this, but I had handled adversity well and had been ahead of Evan, the experienced pro. We did connect again several hours later and shared our final ride of the trip, crossing over onto Mount Desert Island and arriving in Bar Harbor.

It was on that visit that I learned that tides do not operate to the same degree everywhere. I grew up on the Mississippi Gulf Coast, where a normal tide range is two to five feet – high tide can make the water level up to five feet higher than at low tide. In Bar Harbor, the tidal range is closer to twenty or thirty feet. There's even a small island near town that one can walk to at low tide, but it's possible to get stuck out there until the next low tide. It's also apparently possible to get caught mid-crossing and get swept away by the speed of the incoming tide. It certainly made access to certain local swimming holes variable, depending on those incredible swings of the tide.

After a few relaxing days in Bar Harbor, perhaps feeling restless, I decided to set out hitchhiking on my own. Somehow, it made sense to me that I would have better luck if I had a higher purpose. As I'd been thinking a lot about home in reference to tides, I decided to hitchhike from Maine to Mississippi to surprise my mom on our birthday. (And sharing a birthday with your mom is a great motivation to be together.) At that point, I had twelve days to get there. If I hadn't made it all the way by a certain time, I would hop on the bus to finish up the trip.

What could go wrong?

(I mean aside from running across a bridge in the rain, having my guitar case handle break off, barely catching my guitar before it hit the ground, and almost throwing myself in front of a van in the process. But I'm getting ahead of myself, as that was the beginning of ride number two, though it was within scant hours of walking out of sunny Bar Harbor.)

The cross-section of individuals willing to pick up male hitchhikers while driving the Interstates of America in 1993 was somewhat limited. Perhaps a smarter or more cautious person would have suspected this and decided to pay for a bus ticket upfront. With only twelve more days until my 20th birthday – only twelve more days to be a reckless teenager – I was not a smarter or more cautious person. But because of it, I do have a tale to tell .

Day 1: Bar Harbor to Boston

I had, as I mentioned, followed my friend Evan to Bar Harbor, Maine, after camp ended. I wasn't really sure what my plan was next, as I had nowhere I really needed to be until the following winter, when I was reenrolling in college to continue working on my bachelor's degree.

I'd spent a few days in town, hanging out with Evan and his friends, when I decided it would clear my head to explore Arcadia National Park and camp for a couple of days. It was while I was on that camping trip that I hatched my plan to hitchhike to Mississippi to surprise my mom on our birthday.

After another day back in town for preparation, I packed up all my belongings, which were considerable. I carried with me an internal frame hiking backpack with all of my camping gear including a tent, sleeping bag, camp stove with extra fuel, and various foodstuffs; a military surplus duffle bag, almost as large as my hiking pack, filled with assorted clothes and amenities I'd taken with me to have at camp over the summer; and my guitar, contained in one of those cheap paperboard guitar cases with the nylon handle held on with what appeared to be surplus brads from some 1970's middle school English teacher's desk drawer.

Looking back, it may have been a better idea to consolidate my belongings and ship the duffle bag to my destination, but I was trying not to spend money, so I carried everything with me. All in all, I had about sixty pounds of gear in two huge bags plus my unwieldy guitar.

1: On the Road Again

Evan bid me goodbye with a hearty breakfast and assistance carrying my gear to the north end of Bar Harbor, where he left me sitting at the side of Maine's Route 3, the road off Mt. Desert Island. I sat on the side of the road for over an hour, already wondering if this was such a good idea. Car after car passed me by, not even slowing down to get a better look at this over-laden, long haired weirdo trying to hitchhike.

My mind wandered in many directions, trying to decide how long to stay on the side of the road before giving up and heading back into town. I remember deciding several times that, if I didn't get a ride from one of the next twenty cars, or fifty cars, or one hundred cars, that I would throw in the towel. But something kept me out there as each of those milestones passed. I'm a stubborn person, no less so at 19 than I am today. And, after several hours, it finally paid off.

When the small brown Datsun stopped just up the road from me, I was momentarily disoriented. It wasn't until the middle-aged man got out of his car and hollered back at me that I realized I had my first ride. It took a little careful arranging to get my stuff into his tiny car, but I squeezed it all into the backseat and hopped in beside the driver. He told me he was only going as far as Ellsworth, but that would at least connect me to US 1, the highway that would take me southwest to connect with the interstate in Brunswick. I gratefully accepted his short ride, happy to at least be on the road and have my adventure officially underway.

When we arrived in Ellsworth, he stopped at an intersection, and pointed to the left, where US 1 continued west along the town's Main Street. I thanked him and pulled my belongings out of his car. I walked through town and stopped just shy of a bridge. I sat there for a while, trying my luck sticking my thumb out. Once more, time passed in its own fluid way. At some point, I gave up and decided to start walking. I hadn't made it a third of the way across the bridge when the first raindrop fell. I looked ahead and saw some sort of canopy on the far side of the bridge. But before my eyes, a sheet of rain obscured the canopy and started across the bridge to greet me.

I was no stranger to this phenomenon. I could remember as a kid in Mississippi going outside the front door one day to see it pouring rain. Looking out the back door, however, it appeared sunny. I rushed back and forth inside the house a couple of times before heading out the back door and walking around the house to find the spot where the rain started.

2: *Vanagon to the Rescue*

No, a wall of rain was not new to me, but running into one while crossing a slippery bridge carrying way too much baggage *was* new to me. And I didn't think I liked it that much. I started running as fast as I could to cross the bridge and find the canopy I'd seen. I don't think I'd taken ten awkward, ungainly steps before my right hand shot up into the air, suddenly freed from the burden of carrying my guitar. Without thinking, my left hand dropped my duffle and caught the guitar before it could hit the ground. But twisting to catch the guitar, while still running and shouldering a forty pound hiking pack and having just lost the weight I was counterbalancing, caused me to lose what was left of my balance.

I can't tell you the exact sequence of events that followed, but I came to rest sitting on the raised sidewalk of the bridge with my legs in the gutter in front of me. My guitar was in my arms resting on my lap, held tight like a precious child, and the side door of a beat up VW Westfalia was open in front of me. I looked in through the door and saw the smiling, but concerned looking driver staring back at me.

"Wanna lift? Looks pretty soggy out there and I'd hate for your guitar to get wet."

I leaned forward and slid my guitar onto the floor of the bus and unhooked the buckle on my pack's waist strap. I stood and slung it around in front of me to put it next to the guitar. Grabbing my duffle bag, that had come to rest a couple of steps back, I hoisted myself into the back and closed the door.

It took me a while to fully regain my composure, but I had a while, as the couple (I hadn't noticed the woman in the passenger seat before I got in) asked me about my trip. I don't know how coherent my answers were, but the conversation carried along as I took stock of my belongings.

The guitar case was essentially intact, but the handle was gone completely. I pulled a length of parachute cord out of my pack, with my handy roll of duct tape (like the Force, it has a dark side and a light side and it holds the Universe together), and commenced improvising. I ended up with one length of the p-cord duct taped securely to the side of the case, well below where the handle had been, and the other end formed into a loop that could reach over the neck of the case. As the loop slid down and rested near where the body of the case spread out, it both held the case securely closed and formed a sling of sorts that I used as a handle for the remainder of the trip. (A nice bonus was that the p-cord could be hung over a strap on my pack, so I didn't have to carry the guitar in my hands any more. Though I didn't figure that out until a little later in the day.)

As they drove along, I became increasingly tired, especially after warming up from my episode in the rain. I'm not fully sure whether or not I actually drifted off, but I was pulled out of my daze by the sound of gravel under the van's tires.

"This will have to be the end of the line with us. We're headed north from here, and you want to continue that way," the driver said with a wave of his arm to the road out the front window.

I gathered my things and thanked them once again for both saving me from the rain and for helping me get much further along my route.

As they drove off, I started thinking about food and a cup of coffee. I didn't really have time to come to any conclusions, though, as another car stopped nearby within minutes.

3: Gourmet Breakfast?

The small white Subaru was driven by a very friendly and talkative older man. He basically kept the conversation going single-handedly for the next hour or two, drawling in his Downeast Maine accent – with the slight uptick at the end of most phrases.

I know I was told about the history of one town that we passed through, and his experiences as a younger man on a lobster boat somewhere further up the coast. He touched on politics and human nature among a vast array of other topics, but I was having increasing difficulty paying close attention as my hunger was becoming the main focus of my thoughts. Part of me hadn't wanted to accept this ride in the first place because I wanted to get food first, but my experiences waiting so long for the first two rides made it too tempting to pass up. Now that we were well underway, it just seemed rude to ask him to stop.

He finally dropped me off at a gas station situated in a fork in the road – literally, if the fork had three tines, the gas station was the center one. There, he gave me what may have been the best piece of advice of my entire trip. He told me that drivers are much more likely to pick up a hitchhiker if they know the hitchhiker has a specific destination. He didn't think it would really be useful to put 'Coastal Mississippi' on a sign, but he seemed pretty insistent that letting folks know I had somewhere to be would drastically increase my chances with quite a few people.

I thanked him and filed that away for later use, much more intent on getting some food into my system. I headed into the gas station and grabbed a large cup of coffee – the first money I'd spent on my trip thus far. I took that outside and started going through my pack, eventually finding the Cream of Wheat I had from the camp's kitchen leftovers. I scooped the grainy, white powder into my camp mug, poured in some coffee, put a lid on it and swirled it around for a bit. I had to play around with it a bit to find the right consistency, but it made a passable version of food – made even tastier by the bit of hot chocolate mix I added. Looking back on it, it doesn't sound any better than it tasted, but it was food, and I was hungry.

After I ate, I went back in and talked to the clerk for a little bit about the best route to get into Massachusetts. She suggested staying on US 1 until I reached Brunswick, then trying my luck on the Interstate. I might, she indicated, get lucky enough to get a ride all the way to Boston. I thanked her for her insight, and headed back outside to get set up on the side of the road.

After sitting for a while, I pulled out my guitar and played myself a few songs to cheer me up. At some point, I found myself strumming back and forth between the chords D and A, and humming a little melody. Unbeknownst to me, that was the beginning of the song that named this book. ("Ride Collector" is a crappy piece of songwriting, but it was the first song I ever wrote, and it came from the heart, so there's something to be appreciated about it. As long as you don't actually have to listen to it, that is.)

4: *On the Interstate*

While I was playing and trying out some words to go along with my simple melody, a light blue Toyota hatchback pulled out of the gas station and stopped right next to me. The passenger window was down, and the driver was looking at me.

"You the guy headed down to Mississippi?" he asked.

"That's me," I answered, starting to put away my guitar.

"Well, I can't take you that far, but I can get you to the interstate on-ramp in Brunswick, if'n you're ready to go."

I loaded my gear into the back and climbed into the car. He started into a tale from his past about hitchhiking all over Maine back in the day. He indicated that he didn't see hitchhikers all that much anymore, but that he always felt he was obliged to pick up those that he did see as a sort of repayment for all the rides he'd received in his youth. Apparently, he was also a friend of the Subaru driver, who'd been talking about me since he dropped me off.

We chatted amiably for the remainder of the ride down to Brunswick, where, true to his word, he left me at the on-ramp that would take me onto I-295 headed south towards Portland. As I was gathering my stuff, he told me to ask who ever picked me up how far they were headed. He said it wouldn't really be worth it if they were only going as far as Portland because I'd likely get stuck there trying to get out of town. He also echoed the suggestion of the clerk at the gas station, saying that I really ought to have a sign to tell drivers where I was headed.

I thanked him again and shouldered my pack. Walking down the on-ramp, I started scanning the roadside for a stray piece of cardboard that I could repurpose. I knew I had a permanent marker in my pack, so I lacked only something to write on that would withstand the elements to some degree.

Sure enough, I found a discarded cardboard box and took the time to cut off a relatively unscathed section. It was a little over a foot square, and I folded it in half to give it more structural integrity before writing on it, in block letters, "MASS," hoping that drivers would know I was heading to a nearby state instead of a religious event. Once I had that set, I gathered my things again, this time attaching my duffle to the back of my pack and my guitar to the side. With one hand stabilizing the guitar while the other held my sign out to my left for passing motorists to read, I continued walking down the ramp.

5: *Into New Hampshire*

While I may have suspected how useful such a sign might be, I was not prepared for just how effective it was. I had not reached the halfway point of the on-ramp before a huge, white pick-up – the kind with two tires on each side in the back – slowed down and stopped in front of me. The driver got out and reached into the bed of the truck and started rearranging construction materials to make room for my stuff before looking over and asking me where in Massachusetts I was headed.

I explained that I was actually trying to make it all the way to Mississippi, but that I had a friend in Boston that I was going to try to stay with that night. He told me he could get me into New Hampshire, south of Portsmouth, and thought I should be able to get a ride into Boston from there.

Once again, I loaded my stuff into a stranger's vehicle, and we were under way. Unlike my previous two rides, this guy was not very talkative. I tried a couple of times to start a conversation, but his monosyllabic answers made it clear that he was not that interested in sharing deep, personal, meaningful stories with a stranger he found on the side of the road. We passed the time mostly in silence, punctuated by his occasional cursing and lamenting about how poorly people drive.

It was nearing dusk as he dropped me off at his exit, and I started another walk along an interstate on-ramp.

6: *Arrival in Boston*

I did make it to where the on-ramp merged with the highway this time, and decided to stay a bit back from the actual interstate. Passing cars could see me if they were looking, and would have plenty of room to get over and stop if they cared to (as long as there was no traffic trying to enter the interstate at the time). For a while, I held out my sign, almost waving it at cars; however, this felt like it might appear somewhat desperate to drivers, and a desperate hitchhiker is not the kind that most folks wish to pick up.

At some point, I started looking around to see where I might camp for the night if the afternoon deepened much further into evening, but luck was on my side and another small hatchback pulled off of the road and stopped a few hundred feet up ahead of me. I hoisted my pack onto my back and started walking up to meet my newest friend.

I was somewhat surprised when a woman stepped out of the driver's seat when I was still about fifty feet away. She seemed to be studying me very intently, so I slowed my pace and made eye contact with her.

"How far you headed?" I asked.

"Boston," came her reply.

"Well I'm trying to make it to Cambridge to visit a friend of mine at MIT," I told her.

She seemed to nod slightly, to herself or me, and reached into the car to pop the latch releasing the back. I loaded my belongings and hopped in next to her.

Part of me wanted to ask her incredulous questions about why a single woman driving alone at dusk would stop for a male hitchhiker, but that seemed particularly rude, given the kindness she was showing me, and potentially threatening, given the insinuations that would bring to mind. I did spend most of the ride pondering those questions, though, and was somewhat startled when she pulled into a gas station telling me that was as far as she could get me without going too far out of her way.

The yellow lights of the gas station were emitting a faint buzz as I climbed out of her car and dropped my stuff under an overhang near the door of the gas station. The woman filled up with gas, wished me luck, and drove off into the night.

7: Bus Ride

I pulled out my road atlas and started trying to figure out exactly where I was and how to get to MIT. The station attendant showed me where on my map I was, but he wasn't overly helpful with ideas to get me into town. His best suggestion was to call a cab to drive me there, which he said would cost "less than $20." After spending eighty-three cents (on a cup of coffee) to travel 250 miles, it seemed ridiculous to me to spend $20 to travel the last five or so.

I went outside and sat for a while on my pack before I started asking random customers for ideas and suggestions. Several mentioned the bus system, but those that knew it well pointed out I would have to transfer busses two or three times to get to MIT from that gas station. It was after one of these conversations that the attendant came out of the store and started loudly telling me to stop harassing his customers, and that I needed to clear out of there. That turned out to be the best gift he could have given me, because the guy I'd just talked to came back over and offered to drive me over to a bus stop where I could get on a bus that would take me all the way to MIT's campus. I gratefully accepted and soon found myself standing at a sheltered bus stop, waiting for a bus on the correct route. The third bus that came by had the right number on its front, so I climbed on, paid my fare, and confirmed with the driver that he was headed past MIT. Upon hearing his assent, I found a pair of empty seats, put my pack on one seat with my duffle on the floor in front of it and held my guitar in front of me.

Staying attentive to the stops was a challenge after my long day, but I was able to stay focused enough to hop off the bus next to a sign advertising MIT's presence. It was at that point that I realized I hadn't planned very well. It had been months, if not years, since I had seen Kurt. We grew up in the same coastal Mississippi town, but had not stayed in close contact following our graduation and departures for college. (Remember, this is a time when email barely existed, and Facebook was still over a decade from being invented.) I mean, I knew he *went* to MIT, but I had no idea how to find him, and I was quickly coming to see that MIT was a much larger university than the small liberal arts college I attended.

I was able to find a pay phone with a phone book, but it was a Boston phone book, not the MIT-specific phone book I was hoping for. I wandered around for a while before I came across a security office. While it made sense to me at the time to ask there for help, I could quickly tell that they were distrustful of some random stranger showing up in their office claiming to know one of the thousands of students at the school.

They wouldn't give me Kurt's phone number in his dorm room, but they did call him for me. He was a little surprised when he got to the security office to meet me that they simply let us leave. Somehow he'd gotten the impression that I was somehow being *held* by security for some reason.

He led me back to his dorm, where I showered. If memory serves, Kurt gave me the leftovers from the Italian meal he'd gone out for earlier in the evening, and we talked for a while. He told me he'd be able to help me find the right bus to get me to the outskirts of town in the morning, but that he had a class to get to as well, so it would have to be somewhat early in the morning, which was fine with me.

As I recall, I laid down on the short, white sofa in their common room and was instantly asleep.

Wade C Davis

Day 2: Boston to Kutztown, PA

8: Escaping Boston

Kurt helped me find a bus that would get me out to Newton, where I could hook up with I-90 as I headed out of town. I-90 is a toll road, which means that access to it is even more limited than a typical interstate. I ended up climbing under a fence that didn't quite meet the ground next to a bridge that went over the toll road. I scrambled down the dusty bank and found myself on the side of a very busy interstate.

Even that early in the morning, the shade of the bridge seemed to be the best place to wait for my first ride of the day. As it so happened, I had plenty of time to think back over my first day of travel. It seemed that people were in too much of a hurry to get wherever they were going to have any interest in taking a detour out of their daily lives to give me a lift.

I used the time to work on my sign. It seemed the 'MASS' was used up, as I was already in Massachusetts, so I folded the sign over the other way and wrote 'PENN' across it, hoping to find someone headed generally southwest. As the morning rush hour traffic thinned out, I thought that my prospects for a ride were following suit.

It turns out that people leaving the city in the middle of the morning, as opposed to those that fight rush hour, are much more laid back and open to new experiences. Or at least that was the case for the young couple that pulled over for me. She seemed much more enthusiastic about the idea of giving me a ride than he did, and kept saying things like, "We're not going that far, but it has to be easier to get a ride further away from the city."

They took me as far as the far side of Worcester, due to her goading of the poor guy driving that it would be much easier for me to get a ride headed out of town than through town. He grumbled a little about going out of their way, but she either ignored him or reminded him they were not in any hurry. I tried to stay innocuous and quiet in the back seat, to give him as little as possible to object to.

When he finally pulled off the road with a sigh and dropped me at the intersection, she wished me the best of luck and gave me a smile that lasted until they were out of sight. I started what was becoming a familiar walk for me, angling up (or down) the on-ramp towards the cars receding in the distance.

9: *Off the Right Track*

I'll be perfectly honest here, I don't remember these next two rides very well. Or at all, for that matter. Somehow, the events of later in the day superseded these in the recesses of my memory, which I'm sure you'll understand when you read about the last two rides of the day. But as the subtitle of the book points out, there were twenty-five rides, and I'd feel bad as an author if I didn't give you something in exchange for your hard-earned money, so I'll start with the two things I know for sure. I fell asleep on the ninth ride, which is what took me slightly off course and led to the drop-off location of the tenth ride.

Those of you not from central Massachusetts will certainly be able to understand why I may have neglected to remember to tell my ride I was planning to get off the Massachusetts Turnpike in the teeming metropolis of Sturbridge, where I-84 angles down to Hartford, Connecticut. If I hadn't looked it up on Google Maps just now, I wouldn't have known the name of the town either. Those of us who are not from New England have a hard time naming any town west of Worcester in Massachusetts (and we can't pronounce Worcester correctly, in any case – the only time in the English language I'm aware of the letters 'orce' making the 'oo' sound, or at least the Boston version of what 'oo' sounds like). Western Massachusetts is an area chock-full of college towns, but I daresay 90% of Americans wouldn't be able to name a single one of them. (I do mean the towns as opposed to the colleges. I think some of the colleges are quite well known, whether or not I can think of any of them at the moment.) But I digress.

I walked down (or was it up) the on-ramp feeling a

little introspective and sad. I was thinking about the smile that had just ridden away from me and wondering how long the couple would stay together with such different outlooks on life.

I was also thinking about how much better off that woman would be with me as a partner instead of the sourpuss with whom she was driving around. I have a theory that we're all inherently egotistical and tend to believe ourselves to be the single missing ingredient to a successful outcome for virtually any given situation. Or maybe I'm just egotistical on my own – perhaps you don't think that way at all.

In any case, I made it near the end of the on-ramp and started holding out my PENN sign. I have to believe that it took quite some time to get a ride, which would certainly explain why I fell asleep in the car within just a few miles of being picked up. I know that it was a male driver with no passengers because I was in the front seat, apparently sawing logs, when he woke me up to tell me that he was getting off the highway. I asked to be dropped at the beginning of the off-ramp so I wouldn't have to contend with the toll stations.

This, then, became the first ride that I skipped the off-ramp and walked directly on the interstate towards the on-ramp. It happened to be one of the times that the interstate went under a bridge holding the connecting road, so I had a spot to sit in the shade and try to figure out where I was.

10: *A non-connecting interchange*

It was while I was assessing my situation and realizing that it was very likely I'd missed I-84 down to Hartford that my next ride stopped for me. (It was almost amusing after the amount of time and effort I'd put into getting the first two rides that the third ride of the day stopped for me almost before I was ready for them.)

I explained my general situation to the driver as he pulled back on to the highway. He threw a couple of ideas at me, the most logical of which seemed to be for me to get dropped off at the bridge on I-90 that went over I-91, again allowing me to bypass the toll stations. Near Springfield, I exited the Massachusetts Turnpike in early afternoon and scrambled down my second dusty slope of the day. I decided to eat a little in the shade of the overpass, both to pass the time and to keep myself going. Little did I know at the time just how much time I would need to pass.

I ended up pulling out my guitar for a while and working on the few songs I had memorized, as well as continuing to work on my little ditty about hitchhiking. Time still passed agonizingly slowly.

11: *The Grey Ford Ranger*

After sitting on the side of the road under the overpass for two or three hours, I began to feel a little anxious. The thrill of what I'd been doing for the past day-and-a-half had definitely worn off, and I was more than ready to be underway again. Which may explain why, though I felt very uncomfortable about the grey Ford Ranger pick-up truck that pulled up beside me (and its two occupants), I still put my stuff in the bed and stepped up to the cab.

Perhaps it should have been another cue for me to have politely refused the ride when I was offered the center seat; however, I reluctantly (though gratefully) climbed in and watched my new companion climb in beside me. We hadn't even reached highway speed before the passenger slid the window behind my head open and pulled out a beer from the cooler at the cab end of the truck's bed. To his credit, he did offer it to me first, but, after I declined, he handed it to the driver, who popped the can open with one hand and proceeded to drain about half of it from what I could ascertain through the corner of my eye. The majority of my focus remained on the passenger who again reached behind me. I was almost relieved when he pulled forth another beer rather than a club to knock me senseless. Relieved perhaps, but not at ease. I was beginning to realize that my impatience had not served me well. By the time I realized just how deep the shit was that I was sitting in the middle of, the driver had chucked his empty over his shoulder into the bed of the truck, asking for another.

As I was working on breathing deeply to calm my nerves and gain control of my pulse, I began to mentally withdraw from the cab. My mind wandered through the peaceful, Quaker-based camp I'd left behind, thinking about organic food grown there and the lifestyle that accompanied it. It seemed that I was much further removed from that idyllic setting than two days of travel would account for. I started tracing the path that had led me, a former president of his high school chapter of Students Against Drunk Driving, to be riding with two increasingly inebriated individuals.

I was snapped instantly back into the insane reality of my situation when I heard the words 'gun' and 'shoot' in the same sentence coming out of the driver's mouth. It took me a moment to go back in time and reconstruct all of what he had said. (This was one of those moments in life that make one realize just how powerful the human brain can be --

in the moment between hearing those key words and seeing the virtually instantaneous response of the passenger, I was able to loop back and actually listen to the sentence I'd barely heard.)

"Hey, there's one! Grab the gun! I'm going to catch up to them and buzz 'em. You shoot the driver's window."

I was able to get as far in my thinking process to reach a point of incredulity that I'd actually heard such an outrageous phrase when I saw the passenger open the glove compartment. I don't know what kind of sound or movement I made at that point, but the passenger immediately 'reassured' me.

"It's just a paintball gun, see?"

I looked at the small blue, green, and red balls in his hand and, somehow, felt just as much like freaking out as I had moments earlier. Surely what I knew was about to happen was not possibly about to happen. As we passed the minivan they were focused on, I saw a peaceful family – Dad driving with Mom turned back looking into the back seats, where Junior and Little Sister were playing a game. But unlike many of the other cars on the road, this was an African American family.

Surely I haven't gotten far enough in my travels to have reached the overtly racist South. Surely he's not actually going to –

Thoom!

"Damn! I missed! Slow down a little and let them come up behind us – I'll hit their window right in front of the driver."

Thoom!

"Did you see that shit! I nailed 'em! Ha! They're pulling over."

After two more cars were targeted (one was hit in the rear passenger window, while the other was missed entirely), the driver said he saw another one and that he wanted the gun.

I have seen people multitask while driving. (It has bothered me at times, such as watching someone driving a stick-shift, steering with one knee while holding food in one hand and drink in the other.) I have even aided and abetted multitaskers, through both steering and shifting gears, but I had never handed a loaded gun to a drinking driver intent on targeting his fellow motorists. Plus, I didn't want my fingerprints on that thing. But I was sitting in an increasingly perilous situation, and self-preservation took over.

Thoom! Thoom!

Suffice it to say that I was a little nervous about how all of this was going to end for me. Part of me wanted to speak up and decry the injustice and depravity I saw on display. But wouldn't that make me a target, and, even more sinister, a witness who needed to be silenced? I held my tongue, but I'm not sure I hid my reactions.

When they offered to drop me off at an exit ramp, I jumped at the chance, not really looking to see where exactly I was. After they pulled over and I got out, I kept my hand on the truck, just in case they were going to try to zip out of there with my stuff. I quickly unloaded, tossing my pack and duffle on the ground while picking up my guitar. As I stepped away from the pickup, the driver floored it, zipping back into traffic and spraying me with gravel and dust from the side of the road.

Luckily, he had dropped me at a place I could see the interstate signs telling me which road was which, but I had quite a walk ahead of me, following what turned out to not be an exit, but a connector between I-91 South and I-84 West in Hartford. As I began to get a better picture of what I was walking into – it was down into one of the concrete canyons so common for city interstates that I went – I started to wonder if I hadn't just stepped out of the proverbial frying pan. (And if I knew then what I know now about Hartford's reputation as a violent city, I may have been even more worried.)

I sat at the end of the connector ramp, checking my map and trying to figure out any realistic way for me to get out of there. I didn't relish the thought of walking around in the city to find a place to stay, but I also saw no copse of trees to string up a hammock. And it was definitely getting dark.

So far in the trip, this was the definite low point for me emotionally. I felt I had just narrowly escaped a potentially disastrous situation, and had a lot of pent-up emotion surrounding that, but there was no way to express it as I was still in survival mode. I remember holding out my PENN cardboard sign and hoping. But my hope was fading with the daylight, and I have to admit, I was scared. It may have even crossed my mind that I had told no one but Evan (back in Bar Harbor) what I was planning, and, having met him at the beginning of the summer, he knew no one in my family, and my family knew nothing of him. I could disappear out here and no one would have any idea where I was or where I'd gone. Perhaps these were the types of reasons so few people travelled via hitchhiking in the early '90s...

When you're sitting on the side of a road, trying to get a ride, you sometimes feel like you're watching a tennis match from midcourt. You can see cars coming and sometime you think you see a slight drop in the headlights, which might indicate that the car is slowing down. So you'll turn to watch the car recede, hoping that you will, indeed, see brake lights. I do remember my neck getting a little sore while sitting there, looking back and forth, back and forth.

It was while looking again for the tell-tale brake lights that I saw the man at the next entrance, jumping up and down and waving his arms next to his little pickup.

And once again I was astounded at the series of kaleidoscopic emotion that can pass through one person in an instant. Of course there was relief, this was potentially a ride out of this pit of despair. But that was quickly followed by distrust. Why would anyone want to pick up a hitchhiker so badly that they'd park their car and jump up and down to be seen? And if he was on the next entrance up, how had he possibly seen me? No, this had to be a bad thing – this guy was going to try to kill me or rob me or something. Unless he's having car trouble and he needs help. Which would at least give me something to do and someone to talk to while we try to solve his problem, and it might lead to something.

All of that passed in an instant before I even stood up and tentatively waved at him, to see if he was actually waving at me. He stopped jumping and cupped his hands to his mouth. I heard nothing but the cars whizzing by me, but he did wave me over. I figured I had quite a walk to get to him, and I could probably think on the way over, so I shouldered my load and started lumbering along the side of the highway, four lanes of cars zipping past at 65 on one side of me, and a twenty to thirty foot cement wall on the other.

As I got closer, I could see that he was rearranging stuff in the bed of the truck, which had a cap on it. I didn't know if that made me more worried or more trusting, but I kept ambling closer. By the time I could make out his face, he started towards me and offered to carry my duffle bag.

12: *Pennsylvania John*

"Boy, I never thought you'd see me," he said as we climbed into the cab after having stowed my stuff in the back. "I passed you once and tried to loop around and come back for you, but I missed the right entrance and had to get your attention."

"Why go through all that effort," I asked. "Just for a random hitchhiker?"

"Well, that's a long story, but if you're really headed to Pennsylvania we've got a long ride ahead of us. Where are you headed?"

"Mississippi," I replied, "trying to get home for my mom's birthday. But holding up a Mississippi sign seems too far. At least Pennsylvania is in the neighborhood up here."

"Well I can get you as far as Kutztown, which is west of Allentown, if you want to go that far tonight. I figure I'll get home by midnight or so."

"Sounds great to me – I'm just happy to not be stuck in Hartford for the night, and this is a much better option. So, why was it so important to pick me up?"

John's story:
"I came to Hartford today to drop off my step-daughter at college. It's her first year, and it just happened to work out for me to bring her over here. I was feeling a little sad that we won't have any kids at home anymore, and was letting that wash over me when I just barely saw you out of the corner of my eye as I passed you. Seeing you now, it's not so much,

but in that glimpse, you reminded me a lot of my son. That's why I had to try to give you a ride.

"You see, I haven't seen him since his wedding day a few weeks ago. Actually, no one saw him that day, either. He must've gotten cold feet or something, because he just jumped on my motorcycle early that morning and left. We haven't heard from him since. Not us, not his fiancée, no one, as far as I know.

"I guess I can understand how it is for a young man. Looking at committing his whole life to someone at a time he wants to be traveling, exploring, seeing the world. I was like that, too. But you live and learn and, gradually, settling down is more appealing than going out and having adventures.

"Now I don't think anything bad's happened to him, but I want to think that people are looking out for him. If I can't be taking care of him, I might as well take care of another young man, so I decided to reach out. It just fit; it felt right.

"Well, more than that, it felt necessary. Like I had to do it. I was so frustrated when I missed you by a ramp! I sat in the car and honked the horn for a while before I got out and started waving at you. I thought you'd never see me."

Thus started our more than four-hour drive from Connecticut, across eastern New York, and into Pennsylvania. We would take turns talking – about ourselves, our lives, the nature of trust, of belief, of faith in the good in the world – and at a certain point, he encouraged me to get some sleep. He just kept driving quietly through the evening.

I awoke as the truck started to slow. We were getting off the interstate. He pulled into a Denny's and offered to buy me dinner. I tried to politely decline, but he was having none of it. Soon we were seated at a booth, enjoying breakfast for dinner. Conversation was intermittent, and he got up as he finished and went to the bathroom. I saw him as he came out and turned to the payphone. (Some of you may remember those. They used to exist in restaurant lobbies and gas stations.)

He talked over there for quite a while as I finished my meal. He was smiling when he came back over to the table.

"I talked to my wife, and she says it's okay if you stay at our place tonight. I can drive you back out to the interstate in the morning, and you can be on your way again.

"Whaddya say?"

This sounded like the best deal I was likely to get, so I simply agreed. We were back on the road again shortly, and I drifted in and out of sleep for the remainder of our drive.

When we arrived at his home, it turned out their guest room was in the garage, so I had space to myself. I was exhausted, so I pulled out my sleeping bag, rolled up in it, and was asleep momentarily.

Wade C Davis

Day 3: Kutztown to Virginia

I awoke in the morning to the door opening and John walking in with a plate of toast and sunny-side-up eggs for me. After gratefully eating, it was time to get going again. I put my stuff back in the truck and he drove me out to I-78 and dropped me off at the top of the overpass.

I grabbed my gear, expressed my deepest thanks, and tried not to accept the $10 bill he pressed into my hand as he shook it. He told me I was welcome to leave it on the side of the road, but that he was not taking it back, so I might as well use it. (And at this point I suppose I should own up to a potentially misleading element in my subtitle – I did spend $14.40 on my trip, but with this $10, my net expense came out to be $4.40.)

I told him I hoped the best for him and his family. Which is when he smiled and told me that his son had called home after we left the Denny's the previous night. He was on his way back. I do hope that story ended well for all, but as with so many threads in life, I will likely never know. (My mom later sent a thank you card addressed to him in Kutztown, with no street address. I don't know if he ever received it, but I feel pretty confident that from our encounter he received at least as much comfort and joy as I had.)

As John drove off, I once again shouldered my load and started down the ramp to a new day's adventures.

13: Bonnie in the Buick

As it turned out, I barely had to wait for my first ride of the day. I don't even think I got to the end of the on-ramp before a maroon Buick pulled over and I found myself looking for the second time upon a scene I thought I would never see.

There was a woman at the wheel. She was alone in the car. I was so dumbfounded, I think she had to ask me if I wanted a ride. My addled mind gradually caught up with the rest of me as I loaded my bags and guitar into the back seat of the car and climbed in next to her. We exchanged a few pleasantries, and before I could get around to asking her what the hell she was thinking picking up a hitchhiker while driving solo, I realized she was not one of the conversationalists.

I think I've mentioned before that there are essentially two main types of people who pick up hitchhikers. There are those who want someone to talk to, and those who don't. Oh, of course there are many motivations for picking up hitchhikers – I gave people rides every opportunity I had for about ten or fifteen years after these experiences, paying it forward, as it were – but regardless of a person's motivation for pulling over, once the ride is underway, the driver usually makes it pretty clear fairly quickly whether my fare for the ride is entertainment or silence.

It was as I maneuvered the conversation around to a point where I could ask the question burning a hole in my mind that I came to this conclusion. Perhaps it was the monosyllabic answers to any questions I posed. Perhaps it was the pause before answering – too long to be dramatic, too short to be contemplative. Or maybe it was the almost audible sigh of annoyance when I ventured a third or fourth question her direction. Whatever the case, I quickly came to realize that I may never get the chance to gently guide the conversation around to a point where asking the question would be anything but threatening.

"Really, you have family in Hoboken? That's nice. By the way, why would you, a woman driving alone in her car, stop to give a ride to a potential homicidal maniac? Don't you fear for your life, or at least your well-being?"

Because no matter how I phrased the question, that was going to be the subtext hiding between the lines. It wouldn't matter that I'm not a homicidal maniac. Simply asking the question would force that thought into her head, and I'm a polite enough person to try not to make kind strangers offering the world random acts of goodness fear me or the consequences of such decisions.

So I sat, quietly, and watched southern

Pennsylvania pass by my window. As we neared Harrisburg, Bonnie said she was stopping just on the other side of the city. She wanted to know where I wanted to be let off. I told her that it tends to be much easier to get a ride leaving a city than going in to one, and that the far side would suit me just fine. Once again this was greeted with her typical pleasant silence, and I found myself almost eager to be out of this car. Trying not to ask her my question had become difficult almost to the point of being painful for me.

So it was that I was dropped off just south of the Pennsylvania Turnpike where I-81 curves around the south side of Carlisle. There was already evidence of upcoming roadwork, with orange signs and barrels visible in the distance as we took the off-ramp and Bonnie dropped me off before driving into town.

I took a moment at the intersection to check my water bottles and make sure I had my permanent marker in easy reach. It seemed to me that my PENN sign would no longer be useful, so I flipped over the cardboard and wrote VA in large block letters as I walked down yet another on-ramp.

When I reached the point where oncoming cars would be able to see me clearly, I set down my duffle and backpack and decided to pull out my guitar. It had definitely seen some use on the trip so far, but I hadn't played it since the previous afternoon, before my rides into and out of Hartford. (And if the ride *in* was Hell and the ride *out* was Heaven, does that mean Hartford is Purgatory?)

At Farm & Wilderness, the camp I worked at in Vermont before I'd ever hitchhiked anywhere, there is a 'no canned music' policy. This means that, while on camp property, if you want music, you either have to play it yourself or find someone to play it for you.

There are no CDs, no records, no tapes (yes, we still used tapes in the early '90s) – quite simply, no recorded music of any kind.

This had been difficult for me, as I love listening to music. However, as my family had so clearly let me know when I wanted to play saxophone in 6th grade band, I don't really come from a musical family. My friends had a habit of asking me detailed questions about random topics if ever I started singing along with the car stereo. I only realized years later that they weren't interested in my thoughts, but they were very disinterested in my singing voice. And I was gullible and loved thinking that my opinion was valued, so I guess it all worked out for everyone involved at the time.

But as camp wound down for the summer, I had become enamored of the idea that I would learn to play guitar. For me it was as simple as looking at the chord diagram that's above the music and words in many songbooks. Looked like a six by six grid with dots on it to me. I can remember placing my fingers in an arrangement that appeared to be a C chord and strumming. The cacophony of notes that fought with each other to be the first out of the sound hole – presumably to escape the pain of sharing space with the other notes, and to get away from the atonal moron holding the poor instrument – told me pretty clearly that either my family and friends were right and I really had no business even carrying someone's guitar (not to mention attempting to carry a tune), or I had read the chord chart incorrectly. I persevered and tried seeing the diagram with the guitar neck vertically instead of horizontally as I'd first guessed. I strummed again, prepared for the jumble of notes to once again let me know with certainty that I was not to pick up a guitar ever again, but I was awestruck to find that, not only did it not sound horrible, it actually sounded pleasant, perhaps even melodic. In that way I was able to teach myself C, G, D, and A. Which, surprisingly to me at the time, meant I could play about half the songs ever written in the western canon. (Three quarters if you add a capo.)

Granted, I was a halting, rhythmically erratic, semi-tone deaf guitar player, but that was enough for me to have taken my final paycheck from camp and buy my $98 used Epiphone. (Which, I'm quite surprised to say, I still have almost two decades later.)

And it was that very same Epiphone that I pulled out on the side of the road to continue composing my first song. I have to again admit, all these years later, that it was not a very good song:

Oh I'm a ride collector, won't you give me a try
I'm a ride collector, don't you pass me by
I'm a ride collector, you've got nothing to fear
Won't you please stop and pick me up right here.

But the beauty of singing songs, and composing songs, is that time passes. At least that was the beauty for me at the time. I didn't notice how long I sat there, scribbling words into a notebook. In fact, I believe I completely forgot what I was doing, because I remember feeling a little put out when a boxy, pale blue Honda Civic wagon pulled up next to me. I mean, couldn't they see I was busy here? What's the idea of stopping to give a ride to a guy sitting on the side of the road in southern Pennsylvania with a VA sign leaning against his guitar case?

Oh, right. Hitchhiking. That would be exactly what I was writing about and singing about, so perhaps I should be a little more focused on *doing* the task at hand rather than being distracted by *thinking* about the task at hand. In any case, I had to at least look up to see who had stopped for me.

14: *Hippie Elder in a Civic*

She reminded me of the quintessential hippie matron. Clear eyes; long, flowing hair cascading down in multiple shades from pewter to silver; plump, but not so much as to call her overweight; glasses with huge almost square frames rounded off at each corner, resting half-way down her nose; thick strands of beads around her neck and dangling from the rear-view mirror, which also supported a small, handmade dream catcher; a sparse collection of spectacular feathers on the dashboard, beyond which a box of incense rested against the windshield.

Her smile would have warmed up a Minnesotan airport parking lot of cars in January if you could've harnessed it. In fact, I'd loaded my guitar and bags, had a seat, buckled in, and we were on our way before it even occurred to me – another woman driving alone. This simply wasn't supposed to happen. But she was so friendly that I didn't think about it for a while as we slowly made our way through the construction zone.

She talked about stopping to save birds and small mammals that had been hit by cars, nursing them back to health, and releasing them when they'd recovered. She went into amazing detail about an owl she had once saved. Its wing was injured to the point that it couldn't fly, but it still only wanted to eat live prey, so she had to bring in various small rodents to feed it while she gave it time to heal.

She seemed to be a genuinely happy woman. To

the best of my ability to see, this seemed to come from giving of herself to the world without expecting anything in return. She's perhaps the only person I've encountered who actually seemed to be living the life of service espoused by so many of the world's spiritual teachers. Granted, I've never personally met those spiritual leaders, but she felt like I imagined them to feel. Caring. Compassionate. Good.

After we broke through the construction and traffic resumed highway speeds, I decided to ask.

"So, this might seem like a strange or ungrateful question, but why did you, as a woman traveling alone in her car, stop to pick up a hitchhiker?"

She looked at me for a moment, some private joke dancing around in her pupils, and said, as she turned her eyes back to the road, "You felt like a good person. And anyone playing a guitar can't be all bad, anyway."

"Well I thank you," I responded, "for affirming something I believe about myself – that I am a good person – and though I certainly can't claim to be a good guitar player, I'm definitely not all bad."

Our amiable conversation continued as we crossed Maryland, eventually passing over the Potomac into West Virginia. She was encouraging me to remain open to the world and not to allow cynicism to slowly leech away my youthful idealism. Perhaps it's cynical to point out that, a week before my 20th birthday, I (youthfully) believed that my idealism would sustain me throughout my life. Don't get me wrong, as I near 40, I'm still more idealistic than most people I know, but that may say more about the people I know than it says about me. I suppose that I still felt nigh on invulnerable, as many teenagers seem to feel, and believed that invulnerability encompassed my idealism as well, making it unassailable. The thought of losing that fundamental aspect of myself seemed ridiculous, if not laughable.

She seemed to sense this egotism in me and pointed out that blithely believing in a truth does not necessarily make it true. One must work towards truth, and continue laboring to maintain truth. Looking back now, I can see that I misinterpreted her words at the time. When she said 'truth,' I heard 'fact,' which is a very different thing. Perhaps the clearest way I can put it now is that facts don't change – they can be verified. Truth is much more malleable.

One can tell the truth, or only say true things. These are very different, such as when one omits certain details, but still states all information accurately. Political ads have taken this to a whole new level. They'll typically tell you a few true things – facts – and then offer you a 'truth' at the end. But those final truths are often open to interpretation. And, as we all know, two different camps can start with the same facts and come to very different truths as a result.

In any case, her words ring in my ears more true today than they did at the time. For some reason, I'm reminded of a quote from my mom's refrigerator door from when I was in high school. (My sister used it in her high school graduation speech, and it seems apropos.) It went something like, "The point of life is not to be happy. The point of life is to matter. To have it make a difference that you were here at all." On the fridge it was attributed to Prince Somebody-or-other. As I think about it now, through the lens of this wonderful woman, I realize that making your life matter, living such that it matters that you were here, making a difference in the world – that is what gives life meaning. And perhaps happiness comes when you are able to do all of that without caring what your reward will be, and, in fact, expecting no reward or acknowledgement for your actions in the first place.

There is a quote on the dance barn at camp, which I now know is attributable to Khalil Gibran from *The Prophet*. It says Work Is Love Made Visible. A truth, not a fact.

The Civic pulled off the road in West Virginia, and I again thanked this woman whose name I cannot remember. She again shared one of her dazzling smiles, then gently pulled away, heading east, away from the interstate.

As I was not yet technically in Virginia, though I knew I couldn't be too far from the border, I pulled out my cardboard sign, made sure the VA would show clearly, and strapped it to the back of my pack so it would be visible to anyone coming up behind me. I hung my guitar on one side of the pack, hooked my duffle bag on the other side, and began my ungainly amble up the on-ramp.

15: *Red Nissan Makes Me Question Reality*

I made it near the end of the on-ramp and once again set up my bivouac. Backpack and duffle bag leaned against each other, offering me a place to sit, though still keeping me elevated enough to be seen by oncoming cars; guitar case in clear view with VA sign hung on it; and me with my guitar, singing whatever songs I could remember from camp that I also happened to be able to play (still limited to my four chords).

Seems like this was one of the longer waits of the day, giving me time to reflect on topography. Sitting here in 2012, I can simply Google my route and clearly see that I-81 follows a valley that stretches from Pennsylvania all the way at least to Roanoke, Virginia, though it could be argued that it goes beyond Knoxville, Tennessee. At the time, I was thinking that it was odd that, though I could see mountains around me and I knew I was traveling along the Appalachians, there wasn't a lot of up and down on the highway. I knew enough geography at the time to be aware that it was possible to travel essentially parallel to the ridge lines – the Appalachian Trail did this from Georgia to Maine, primarily following the actual ridgelines, though.

Having family in the mountains of North Carolina, I have always associated that state with the Appalachians, irrespective of my knowledge that they stretch all the way from Georgia to New England. Having just spent my summer in Vermont and having hiked sections of both the Appalachian Trail and the Long Trail while there, I was much more astutely aware that I should, at this point in my travels, be well within that ancient mountain range. Looking at the scenery around me though, I decided that it would make no better sense to have a hiking trail running along the valley floor than it would to have an interstate along the ridge lines. Somehow, while being solidly within my favorite mountain range, I felt I was missing it completely. In some sense, I wanted to pay closer attention to the land through which I traveled instead of focusing so deeply on the people offering me passage.

Which ended up working out quite nicely when the driver of the red Sentra turned out to be one of the quiet drivers. She pulled over as she was coming up the ramp, stopping just before she got to me. She leaned out the driver's side window and asked me where in Virginia I was headed.

"Wytheville," I said. "From there I'm headed south to visit my grandparents."

I'm not sure exactly what made those words come out of my mouth, but something told me that she wanted me to have a specific destination, but that going into my whole story about Maine to Mississippi for a birthday visit would be too much. I guess I decided she wanted to give me a ride, and this was her way of testing to see if I was a real traveler or a raving lunatic.

Whatever the case, she told me to toss my stuff in the back, which I did before climbing into the front seat beside her. I tried making small talk – asking her where she was from, where she was headed, what she did for a living – but kept getting terse answers, as if I were making her nervous. So I quickly gave up and looked out the passenger window, watching my beloved mountains flow by.

At times they seemed like they were going to come close enough that I would be able to reach out and touch them, while other times the peaks almost disappeared beyond the horizon of the wide valley. I began to imagine that I was traversing the land on foot, running along the ridgeline at blinding speed.

I must have gotten overly drawn in to my own daydream, because I felt myself awaken as the car began to slow. Opening my eyes, I could see we were exiting. And that's one of the problems with falling asleep in someone's car – you have no idea how far you've traveled. Was it ten minutes or two hours? I had no idea, but I did feel that leaden, post-nap cloudiness. And it never occurred to me to ask the woman why she'd picked up a hitchhiker. Perhaps it was just my lot in life to be a good person and to be picked up by good people, at least most of the time.

As she drove off, I realized that my ride prospects

would be difficult from this point. There was a low peak at this exit that the oncoming traffic had to curve around. Just as they would come out of the shadow of the peak, getting hit with full sunshine, I would also come into their view. Only people who were paying close attention would even notice me. Well, them and those entering the highway. But judging by the size of the interchange, cars entering the highway were going to be pretty rare.

16: Magnum

Sadly, I was right. I sat at that interchange for several hours as the sun gradually starting sinking in the sky. This added to the problem of being seen as the sun continued to be more and more at my back. At a certain point, if I were still there in the evening, I realized the sun would frame me in the driver's view, making me completely impossible to see.

I began to feel forlorn.

Sad.

Lonely.

Possibly even desperate.

I started to feel trapped as I looked around and didn't see any accessible place to string up a hammock or even curl up under a tarp. Somehow, in the lush southern Appalachians, I had found a desolate space. And it seemed the longer I stayed there, the more that desolation settled into me.

I tried playing my guitar, but I couldn't think of anything to play. Words to songs were escaping me, as were chord progressions. I put the guitar away again. For the third time.

I'm coming to realize that it may not be possible to

convey on paper the mind-numbing boredom that accompanies hitchhiking. Sure there will be stories to tell when the trip is over, but the interesting and worthwhile stories cover less than one percent of the duration of the trip. The rest of it, as I alluded to in the foreword, is the boredom of sitting on the side of the road, or the tedium of sitting in a stranger's car. And, when a driver is particularly reticent, the difference between the side of the road and the inside of a car is negligible.

Perhaps I dozed again. I certainly hope so, because sitting in one place long enough to notice the sun's progression across the sky gets old, and I would prefer to think that I at least got some sleep.

In any case, I was more than ready to take whatever the world offered me in terms of a ride by the time the black Datsun pickup with gold trim rolled to a stop. The middle-aged black man at the wheel hollered through the open passenger window for me to toss my stuff in the back. As I finished that, the door swing open for me, pushed by a hand that, as it moved back across the seat, was sweeping a bunch of Magnum condoms out of the way.

Now my stuff is already in the truck, and I'm at the open door, trying to wrap my mind around what I've just seen. *Were those really condoms?* (Glance to the floor and the arm rest.) *Yup, those are really condoms.* Magnum? *Aren't those supposed to be the large-sized condoms, for well-endowed men?*

"Well come on... Get in," he said with a touch of impatience.

Well at least I know that I'm clearly communicating my hesitation. I slowly sat down in the seat, pushing a few stray condoms out of my way. He apologized, grabbed them and opened the armrest, where I could see a sea of condoms. He dropped the strays in and closed the lid.

We start to pull into traffic and made some of the most awkward small talk that it's ever been my displeasure to participate in. Or perhaps that was just me – he seemed pretty relaxed, all things considered. I do not recall feeling at all relaxed. I was already starting to berate myself for not getting a sense of the situation before throwing my stuff into his truck. Wasn't this the same mistake I'd made while heading south into Hartford? Jump into the first car that stops after you've been stuck somewhere a while? We can see where that leads. Hitchhiking is known as a dangerous and foolhardy thing for a reason, you know. And here I was, up to my neck in one of those reasons. Again.

Before too long, he turned to me just a little.

"'Fore I stopped to pick you up, I was doin' something. You mind if I finish?"

Flabbergasted would be an appropriate word at this point, but is there a word for flabbergasted squared? Or cubed, perhaps? But add healthy doses of dismay and discomfort, plus a dash of 'he didn't just ask that!' for good measure.

"I, uh, think that would make me pretty... uncomfortable," I think I said.

Silence. Irritated, indignant silence.

"No. You cain' jus do that. I'm here drivin' my own car and I'm givin' you a ride and you're gonna tell me I cain' finish what I was doin' 'fore I stopped for you.

"That's crazy. That's bullshit is what that is."

"Then why don't you just drop me off at that exit coming up? I don't want to keep you from doing anything; I just don't want to be here when you do it."

"Well fine, then! I will. I'm stoppin'. You get out and I'll do what I damn well please!"

He didn't seem really angry, per se, but he was

definitely indignant. That suited me just fine, as all I wanted in the world at that point was to get out of his car and sit on the side of the road by myself and calm down.

He quickly pulled over, still a ways from the actual off-ramp, and I got out. Again, I kept my hand on the truck, ready to dive in after my stuff, or grab it all out and throw it to the side quickly, but he let me grab everything without further drama.

I think he said a few choice words as he drove off, but I was too happy to be back on my own to really notice.

I sat there and collected my wits for a minute or two before starting to gather my bags again. Being in Virginia at this point, my VA sign seemed kind of useless, but the PENN side gave me an idea. I blacked out the top of the P, adding equal marker on the other side of the letter, turning it into a T with a very thick top. I tucked my TENN sign into the back of my pack, attached the guitar and duffle, and walked uphill towards the exit ramp.

As I started curving away from the interstate, I saw that the interstate went underneath at this interchange. Both to shorten my walk and to have the advantage of the shade under the bridge, at least momentarily, I decided to stay on the highway as I walked to the other end of the on-ramp.

As I walked along, I kept debating with myself if I'd actually been in any danger just now, or whether it was just a weird experience. Nineteen years later, I still don't have a good answer to that question. Though, in retrospect, it does seem odd that Magnum-Man was the only male who'd stopped for me all day. A trend that was about to continue.

As I neared the underpass and the shade that I sought, I could faintly make out the sound of a decelerating car behind me. But it was the iconic sound that made me turn around. And sure enough, there was a VW Bug starting to pull off the road as it neared me.

17: Chicks in a VW Bug

As they pulled up next to me, I could see two young women in the car. But if you've ever been in one of the old Beetles, you know how small they are, and this one was already packed with stuff. I guessed they were headed back to school for the fall, which turned out to be accurate.

Rachel, in the passenger seat, hopped out and started putting my guitar in the back, on top of a pile of stuff she scooted over behind the driver, before climbing back there next to it herself. It was then that they noticed the duffle bag.

Now my hiking pack is a full sized, internal frame pack. Fully loaded, as it was at the time, it stands well over three feet tall and is about two feet wide at the base, tapering gradually to be closer to a foot at the top.

The duffle bag is a standard army issue canvas cylinder, where the top folds in and there's one clip to hold it closed. It's almost as big as my pack, but I packed it much lighter, since I was frequently carrying it. Rachel told me to pass it back to her, which I dubiously did. She simply plopped in on her lap and pulled the seat back so I could get in.

Now I'm not a tall guy (five foot eight, if you must know), but squeezing into the front seat, pulling my pack on to the floor between my feet, and shutting the door took considerable flexibility and creativity.

Again, not knowing the reader's familiarity with the VW Bug, I'll let you know that they don't typically have too much power. It's not a muscle car. I'd been in Beetles with three passengers, and it could take a bit to really get moving. But we were three passengers, accompanied, as far as I could tell, by all of our worldly possessions. We were facing uphill, and it seemed like the engine was racing to get us to gradually start rolling forward. The hill leveled out as the entrance ramp met it, by which point we might have been doing 20 miles an hour.

Still, once that little car got up to speed, it seemed strong and stable enough, with the signature thrum of the engine following us along. They asked me about my trip, and I told them where I'd started and where I was headed. They confirmed my earlier guesses about their destination, and we talked as we rode along.

I believe I told them my reason for taking time off from school – getting caught moving a ten foot tall insect makes for a pretty good story, especially when embellished in person – and I was feeling pretty good.

Before too long, during a lull in conversation, Rachel asked from the back seat, "You wanna smoke?"

"Oh, no thanks," I replied, "I don't smoke."

There was a silence for a few moments. A mile marker passed by my window. Thinking back on it now, I can only imagine the series of looks that was going back and forth through the rear view mirror. You see, there are times in my life I've been very dense and unobservant. But I do know I was spending more of my time looking out the window than I was looking over or back to engage these women. Keep in mind, I had just gotten out of that little black Nissan pickup that had rattled me. I hadn't even gotten to the next entrance ramp to set up shop and start looking for another ride. I was still semi-shell-shocked.

But again, at the time I thought it very polite for Rachel to have climbed in the back. (Certainly the guys in the pickup headed into Hartford hadn't been that polite.) Perhaps, though, it was a way for them to be able to communicate with each other while I was in the car. Unless I was looking at one or the other of them, they certainly had eye contact with each other at any given moment. And, as I mentioned, I spent most of my time looking out the window.

"You do know we mean weed, don't you?" said Rachel from the backseat.

If I'd been distracted by my immediate past prior to this moment, I was pulled into the present completely. I turned back and looked at her and saw Rachel was holding a small, wooden object. As I watched, she turned the top of it, which spun horizontally out to reveal a bowl with a little green bud within it.

"Well, in that case," I responded, "why didn't you say so?!"

The mood in the car got very animated and mellow over the next few minutes. My sense of time evaporated. I let go, or thought I did, of my worries and insecurities and let the Bug carry me into the early evening. Laughter punctuated the miles, and we enjoyed both raucous storytelling and pristine silences.

At some point, Stephanie, for that was the driver's name, said that their exit was coming up. Did I want to come with them and stay the night, or should they let me off at the exit?

There are moments in life that you look back on and wonder what was going on in your mind. Why would you make that decision? How would life be different today if you'd picked the door on the left?

I'm not talking about the major decisions that affect the entire course of your life – your major in college, where to live, what to do for a living – but rather the small but poignant moments when you wish you'd made the other choice. Unlikely, perhaps, to change the course of your life, but certainly offer you another worthwhile story to tell, beer in hand, around a campfire someday.

This was such a moment. Even at the time, I can remember looking at myself incomprehensibly as I saw and heard myself say, "Go ahead and let me off at the exit. I can probably get a couple more rides today. I've got a long way to go to get home."

What kind of a moron was I? Two attractive young women with weed, offering to take me home and put me up for the night. More than likely, there'd be dinner somewhere in there, and maybe some drinking – who knows, I might not even sleep alone. But I just turned that possibility down without more than a moment's thought.

I blame Magnum Man. He threw off my balance. He spiked my creepy meter, and now I was stoned on top of that. Whatever judgment I had was pushed to the straining point. (And remember, this is the same questionable judgment that had me deciding it was a good idea to hitchhike over eighteen hundred miles to surprise my mom on our birthday.)

Whatever my motivation, they did let me off at the exit, asking more than once if I was sure. For some reason, I was sure. And as they drove off and I started down the on-ramp again, I looked very closely at the grove of trees off to the side of the road, perhaps instinctively aware that was going to be my resting place for the night.

I did give it the old college try, mind you, but by the time most cars had on their headlights, I knew I was done for the day. I hauled my bags back to the grove and walked into it. Once I was hidden from the traffic and interchange lights, I set my stuff down and kicked myself for about the four thousandth time. As I set up camp, everything I experienced was mentally compared to an increasingly idealistic vision of what I had turned down.

As I strung up my hammock, I thought about a couch that I could be sleeping on. As I gnawed on my hunk of bread and chunk of cheese, I thought about a pizza, with cheese dripping over chunky toppings. When I washed my meal down with water that had been in my bottle since early that morning, I thought about a crisp, cold beer. As I climbed into my sleeping bag, I thought of a soft, fuzzy blanket. And as I fumbled my way into the hammock, I thought about lying down on a soft mattress, with Rachel's laugh still in my ear.

Needless to say, I lay, gently swaying back and forth in that hammock, for a long time that night as I reviewed the choices I had made that day, and the choices that had made me. I vowed not to accept any more rides that made me even slightly nervous or wary – it's just not worth it. I had two icky stories to tell, which was an excellent outcome for either situation. Things could have been much worse. But I also vowed to follow the flow more, too – tonight, for example, things could have been much better.

In retrospect, this particular experience may have strongly influenced my twenties. That was the decade in which I grabbed life by the throat and savored experiences fully – both the joys and the pains.

I believed then – and may still, who really knows? – that people can either experience joyous highs in their lives and the tumultuous lows that accompany them, or they can remain much more even keeled. Essentially, the idea is that one does not have the capacity for happiness without sadness, joy without pain, ecstasy without despair – there must be a balance. But I also believe that one can either temper oneself or throw fuel on one's own flames. In my twenties I lived a life of great joys and great sorrows – I made conscious choices to 'live life to the lees' as Tennyson wrote of *Ulysses*. That line has walked with me throughout life, from the very moment I was forced to look up what 'lees' were when I asked in class. (And my high school English teachers should be credited both with me knowing the poem and for making me think about it – and many other things – deeply.)

As I near my forties, I choose to follow a less tumultuous path. I still drink life to the lees, but my tea leaves tend to be less bitter now than they once were. There are still ups and downs, but rarely the emotional highs and lows that I experienced as a younger man.

Such as the low I experienced while I was lying in my sleeping bag, cursing myself soundly for turning down a place to stay for the night in the interest of trying to get just a few more miles down the road. There may have been some blubbering and crying, too, but we're going to leave young Wade to his pity party and move on to the following morning.

Day 4: Virginia to Tennessee

When I awoke the following morning, I felt refreshed, both through having sleep, but also because the feeling of missing out on something had passed. Wherever else I *might* have awoken that morning, I was now in the best location to continue my travels. I took my time breaking camp. I boiled water, both for oatmeal and for tea, and enjoyed myself as the birds called through the trees (and the occasional semi passed less that forty feet away).

Who knows, I might have even used the last of my water to give myself a minor sponge bath. Stranger things have happened. In any case, the sun was already clear of the horizon before I hauled my gear down to the side of the highway and began courting drivers.

My mind continued to puzzle through the mystery of the previous day's female drivers, though I think I focused on that more to keep my mind off the previous day's sole male driver than to come to any conclusions about why so many women had given me a ride. And, while I did ponder whether this day would continue the trend, the bearded face in the window of the Jeep slowing down for me made me think it would not, at any rate, start off that way.

18: Getting started

Jeff (or was it Geoff – I didn't ask) was on his way to work and was therefore not traveling very far, but I told him that any progress down the road was helpful. If nothing else, it would break up the monotony of my morning.

We cruised along for about fifteen or twenty minutes before he asked where I wanted to be dropped off. Since I'd used the last of my water, I said the gas station would be great. He pulled in and helped me unload before he continued on his way.

I went into the gas station and washed my face and hands before filling my water bottles. I always feel a little guilty using the facilities at a place of business without making a purchase, but there wasn't really anything I actually wanted. I did grab a cup of coffee, just for appearances sake, before heading back outside.

I'd taken inventory before packing up that morning, so I knew I had enough food to make it through the day, especially if I chose to take a break at lunch and do a little cooking on my camp stove. I shouldered my pack, attaching my duffle and guitar to keep my hands mostly free, and carried my coffee down the entrance ramp.

Once again, it didn't take long before an older Oldsmobile pulled up next to me. This was one of the few times that a car coming down the on-ramp stopped for me – usually my rides came from cars already on the highway.

19: *Connections to Wytheville*

After loading my gear into the back seat of David's Olds, I hopped in the front with my still steaming cup of coffee.

"D'ya bring some for me?" David asked with a smirk on his face.

"No, sorry," I replied, "but I'm willing to share."

"Nah, I'm just joking. You drink your coffee, I've already had mine."

We settled into a comfortable conversation about weather and mountains, sharing stories from our childhoods. He'd grown up in the mountains of southwestern Virginia, while I'd spent my summers visiting my grandparents in the mountains of northwestern North Carolina. Several times we found ourselves taking about places the other knew of, and once or twice we found we'd been to the same places and had similar experiences.

Tweetsie Railroad near Boone, North Carolina was one such place. When I was a boy, my grandparents had taken my sister and me there for a fun day, but we'd gotten distracted by all the fun to be had and were separated from them. When my grandfather finally found us, I was waiting for my sister to be done with a mini roller coaster ride. He gave me an earful about being careful and checking in, but his bluster had faded by the time my sister got off the ride, so she didn't feel the brunt of his angry concern.

David had also wandered off from his family there, though in his experience, he was the one who was scared and upset when he couldn't find his family.

Stories such as these helped pass the miles and gave me a feeling of warmth and belonging. So much so that I was saddened when David began to slow the car and exit from the highway. But as we traveled down the ramp, I realized that things looked vaguely familiar to me, though I didn't figure out exactly why for quite some time.

As David pulled away, I waved goodbye and optimistically set out immediately to head up one of the steeper on-ramps I'd seen. I was tired by the time I reached the top, so I was not, at first, bothered by not getting a ride right away again.

But minutes gave way to hours as the sun continued to climb higher in the sky. After what I guess was about an hour and a half sitting in the same spot, occasionally playing guitar, and watching hundreds of cars disappear around the bend in the road, I started to get impatient. I decided to head back down to the gas station and take a break.

While I was down there, I pulled out my atlas and realized why this interchange looked familiar. I was in Wytheville, at the intersection of US 21 and I-81. I realized that my grandparents, both sets, lived about an hour and a half down the road. While this was a nifty realization, it also set my mind against itself for the next hour or more.

Part of me was resolute that I would continue traveling west, hitchhiking my way home, while another, increasingly strong part of me wanted to simply pack it in and call my grandparents, tell them where I was, and see if they'd come pick me up. I know I picked up the pay phone at least fifteen times with the thought that I was going to make the call, but each time I realized that it would not just be a visit with family. It would also be the end of my exploits, as there would be no way I could get them to drive me back out to the interstate to continue hitchhiking.

I debated with myself while standing at the gas station. I debated with myself while walking back up the on-ramp. The internal debate raged on as I stood, TENN sign in hand, trying to get someone to stop for me.

In many ways, and despite the two particularly bad rides I'd had over the past two days, sitting at the top of that steep on-ramp was the absolute low point of my trip. It was definitely the only place that I very seriously considered throwing in the towel. (Sure I thought about it other times, but there was never such a clear second option that made the thought more than idle speculation.)

After another long bout of interminable waiting accompanied by internal wrangling, I again descended to the gas station. This time I made myself some lunch, relaxed my mind by realizing that I didn't have to make any actual decision until much later in the afternoon. I did go so far as to look in the phone book to figure out if there was a bus station that might offer a way for me to get down to West Jefferson to visit my grandparents without needing them to come to me, but I couldn't find anything.

It occurs to me now that this was one of the few times in my life I've been totally on my own – with no one knowing where I was or what I was doing. Throughout the trip, I made no phone calls and had no communication with anyone I had known before, aside from Kurt at MIT. Surprisingly, there was neither a sense of fear (except at specific moments) nor the expected sense of freedom. It was drudgery. A long, endless, monotonous trek, punctuated by long or short walks on highway ramps.

I again shouldered my gear and took another of those walks, this one for the third time on the same, steep on-ramp, and set up my stage at the top of the hill. This time I had my guitar out, and had my TENN sign both visible and reachable. When a car came along that I thought looked particularly promising, I'd grab the sign and hold it up a little higher.

Once again, this went on for quite some time, but I did enjoy myself a little more as I played music and made up words and waved at drivers. I can't say for certain whether I waved or held up my sign to the GMC full-sized pick-up, but the maroon and grey truck pulled alongside me and stopped with its bumper even with my gear.

20: *Pick-up across the border*

The grizzled man got out and started walking back around the truck to me. He seemed to size me up as he walked around.

"I'm only just crossing the border, but I'll get you that far. After all, anyone who plays guitar can't be all bad."

I thanked him and he helped me put my gear into the bed of his truck, paying attention to making sure nothing would blow or shift around. Being the first person who'd taken that kind of care of my things, I thought it was touching. Not the kind of thing I would have expected out of... – but then, you can't judge a book by its cover.

Dan was a jack of all trades, by trade. The stories

he told me of the things he'd built, projects he'd worked on, trips he'd taken were full of details of the challenges he faced and how he used materials creatively to not only make things function, but to also make them aesthetically pleasing. I needed only add a 'really,' a 'yes,' or a 'how?' every once in a while to keep up my end of the conversation.

As we neared the border, he asked a little about me. It sounds amazing, but somehow the phrase, "I'm taking time off from college and hitchhiking down to surprise my mom for her birthday," when spoken as truth, has an effect on people.

Dan almost immediately opened up. Broadened. Deepened. (Funny, I'm a writer, but I can't find a word to express what happened.) In some way, he suddenly seemed to care what happened to me. Not in any creepy way – he just seemed to resonate with a chord of humanity that compelled him to do what he could for me.

He started by saying, "I'm not really just crossing the border. I'm going all the way to Nashville. That's almost three hundred miles from here, so it'll take a few hours.

"Why don't you get some sleep? I'll wake you up when we need to stop for gas."

The conversation continued for a bit after that, but I did continue to get more comfortable. I don't know exactly how long it was before I fell asleep, or how long I was asleep. It was sometime in the early evening when I woke up. The sunlight, diffuse through the clouds, was definitely waning.

I didn't really move when I awoke. Either that time or the next. And I'm not sure I was awake for long, but I did find myself brooding over the nature of safety, related still to the women who had given me rides the previous day. I pondered what would be different if any of them were on this trip in my place? Would there be any possible way they would be safe? I guessed they might get rides faster, but that didn't necessarily promise safety. How would the Paintball gunners have treated a female hitchhiker? Or Magnum Man, for that matter. It seemed to me that being male immediately offered me greater security in this society. I'm not saying that men are never at risk, but I certainly felt more safe on my trip than I believed I would have felt (and experienced) if I were a woman.

I drifted into sleep again for a bit. This time, when I awoke, it was mostly dark out. My brain continued its internal dialogue.

How would it be different if I were not white? So far, all but one of my rides were Caucasian drivers. How many of them would have given me a ride if I'd been black, or Latino, or Native American? I guessed some, but certainly not most. Would a hitchhiker receive rides predominately from people of his or her own race? The possibility was there, but I somehow doubted that there would be a peer-reviewed study of the issue coming out anytime soon.

What struck me, though, in all of this was what I perceived to be a very clear, concrete example of something we'd discussed in one of my courses in college. There'd been discussion on the concept of White Male Privilege, and an abstract dance around what it meant and how it influences people's lives, but there'd been a lack of specific examples of actual situations in which a race or gender change would likely lead to a different result. (Hard, perhaps, to get a bunch of 18 year olds talking about such things in a concrete way – we 18 year olds think we own the world and can effectively deal with any situation – ahh, the immortal teenager.)

White Male Privilege was allowing me to hitchhike from Maine to Mississippi with no apparent malice or ill-will directed at me throughout the whole trip. Again, not that it would be impossible for a black woman to make the same trek, but the realities of our society would likely make that a very differently toned memoir.

I must have drifted off again, because he woke me about a half mile from an exit. We stopped at a gas station and he began filling the truck. After a quick bathroom break, we were on our way again. We were also nearing Nashville.

When he asked what would be best in terms of where to drop me off, I told him that my first choice would be somewhere outside of the interstate loop on the far side of town, and my second choice would be outside of the loop on the near side of town.

"Well then, you get your first choice. I live on the far side of town, about twenty miles out."

"Perfect, and thanks!"

We rode primarily in silence for the remaining half hour of the drive. He seemed a little hesitant to drop me at the actual intersection, so I let him drop me at a McDonald's next to a Motel 6. He was welcome to reach whatever conclusions he needed to in order to drive away, leaving me there, in the dark, alone.

As soon as he was out of sight, I walked back up the road and found a meager stand of evergreen that I hoped would still hide me from traffic come morning. I didn't bother unpacking much – just my sleeping bag and hammock. I barely remember lying down. But I was up bright and early, just before the sun peeked over the horizon.

Wade C Davis

Day 5: Tennessee to Starkville, MS

I gathered my gear together pretty quickly, seeing how little I had unpacked the night before. I was glad I'd woken up so early, as I realized that I would be perfectly visible to anyone who drove by, especially with my royal blue sleeping bag dangling in the trees. I came out of my paltry grove and decided to treat myself to breakfast. I'm not sure just how far north they reach, but I was happy to see the yellow squares that comprise the sign for a Waffle House.

I ambled over to the diner, walked in, and took a seat by a window. I piled my gear across from me in the booth. I had coffee. I ordered my hash browns scattered, smothered, and covered. (Those of you familiar with Waffle House will know exactly what combination of cheese and vegetables I enjoyed; the rest of you will have to look up their menu online if you're that curious.) I savored my meal.

As I was eating, a guy waved at me from outside the window. He pointed at my gear and in a sort of pantomime, asked if I was hitchhiking. I nodded yes, and he started towards the door. How he had figured that out just by looking at a backpack bewildered me until I realized my TENN sign was clearly visible through the window. Lucky placement, I guess.

21: My lucky Waffle House

Joe came in and introduced himself, at first he seemed apologetic for interrupting my meal, but he asked me where I was headed. I told him my plan to surprise my mom for her birthday, which meant I was still generally headed west. He seemed happy to hear that, saying he was headed that way, too. He offered me a ride, but let me know that he hadn't eaten yet, so I'd have to wait a little before we got on the road.

That seemed fine with me, so he sat down and we started talking. Turns out, he'd done some hitchhiking earlier in life and was always happy when he could give someone else a ride. That provided us with fodder for more hours of conversation than we had at our disposal, but we continued talking as he paid for both of our meals, loaded my stuff in his little Subaru, and headed down the road.

One of my favorite stories of his was from when he was hitchhiking from San Francisco up to Olympia. He'd been on the road for a day and a half and was in southern Oregon. A minivan full of people pulled over. He didn't notice anything odd at first, but when they opened the door, he realized that none of them were wearing any clothes. They all had something draped over their torsos – shawls, towels, unbuttoned shirts – but when they opened the door, most of them tossed their coverings aside. They explained they were nudists on the way from one resort to another and had decided as a group not to change for the trip. And they made his accepting a ride conditional on his disrobing for the journey.

"I told 'em I'd been on the road for a day and a half, but they said they could open some windows – hell, they were already open. So I dropped my pack on the floorboard, folded my clothes neatly and stacked them on top, set my boots beside the pack and climbed in. One of 'em even asked me if I had something to throw on quickly if we were going to be visible to anyone.

"I pulled out my towel – always gotta have a towel, right? – I pulled out my towel, set it on my clothes, and we were on our way."

He said he stayed with them at the nudist camp for three days before continuing on his trek. The most amazing part to him, in retrospect, was that he totally forgot everyone was naked after about twenty minutes in the car and within an hour of arriving at the retreat. It was only when he was putting on his clean clothes three days later that it occurred to him again.

Joe was apologetic again as he pulled off the road.

"I'm sorry I can't take you any further, but this is my exit."

I assured him that it was fine, that I appreciated the company, the conversation, and the breakfast. I grabbed my bags out of the back and watched him drive off before crossing the road and starting down the on-ramp to whatever adventure was next.

22: *Every mile counts*

I believe I made it only about halfway down the entrance ramp before a beat-up old Ford Ranger pulled alongside me. The driver's beard was easily as big as the rest of his head, but there was definitely a smile hiding in there somewhere. I could see it in and around his eyes much more clearly than I could see his mouth.

"I'm only goin' two exits up, but I figure that's about two exits further than ya' are right now, so that oughta do ya' good." Still no mouth visible, but there was clearly one in there somewhere.

I'm only guessing about this, but I think it's rare for a hitchhiker to feel frustrated by getting a ride so quickly. Especially after my experience in Wytheville the day before, I really couldn't believe myself, but sure enough, right there inside me, was a disappointment that I really didn't understand or appreciate. I know I'd been thinking about getting to the end of the ramp and setting up shop again – maybe play a little guitar – but to be upset with this happy, bushy man for offering me a ride? What was wrong with me?

I did accept his hospitality, and tossed my stuff in the bed of the truck before pulling on the door handle.

"Ya gotta pull up while you open it. Door sags a bit."

I had only been pulling out, but as the door cleared the edge of the car, it began to drop. I tightened my grip considerably and hoisted the door open. Bolted to the inside of the door near its base was a thick, leather strap handle that I realized later was the end of an old belt.

"Get around on this side and hold up on that 'til

ya' get in. She's a bit persnickety, but she gets me where I need to go."

I climbed in and pulled the door closed, feeling more than a little uncomfortable with the grinding noises that made it hard to hear when the latch engaged. When I'd pulled it to the point I guessed was fully closed, I started reaching for the seatbelt.

"Hey, pull on that handle," he said, pointing at the inside door latch. As I reached to pull on it, he leaned over me and grabbed the leather handle. He whipped the door outward about an inch or two, which yanked the handle out of my hand. In the same motion, he lifted up and yanked the door closed with a resounding thud, almost drowning out the sound of grinding metal accompanying it.

As he sat back, I wondered briefly if I was going to be able to get the door open in two exits, but I figured I'd deal with that later. He crammed the gear shift into first and slowly let the clutch out while revving the engine. We slowly picked up speed, assisted by the downhill slope, and were possibly approaching highway speed by the time we cleared the exit ramp.

"I figure ya' got about ten or fifteen minutes 'fore I drop you off again, so ya' better get started," he said through his thick beard. I could just make out his mouth when looking at him in profile. "Where're ya' from, where're ya' headed, an' what's yer story?"

Given a prompt like that, I figured I'd better start at the beginning, which, in this case, was also the end.

"Well I'm from coastal Mississippi, which is where I'm headed," I started, "to surprise my mom for her birthday." I continued to tell him about my summer in Vermont and the string of events, edited for brevity, that led to his stopping for me moments earlier.

He threw in various noises, from the guttural to

the wistful, with all of the 'ah's, 'uh-huh's, and 'mmm's' in-between, letting me know he was listening and encouraging me to continue. My story and his punctuation continued all the way to the bottom of the exit ramp he took. He pulled to the side and reminded me that it would take two hands to get the door open, suggesting that I grab the strap with my right hand and push the door with my shoulder while pulling the latch. As the door ground open, broke free, and sagged, he thanked me for an entertaining yarn and wished me well.

"Yer mom know yer doin' this?" he asked as I maneuvered around the door to the outer handle.

"No," I replied, simply.

"Good! She'd have a heart attack if she knew what yer up to. When ya' get home, tell 'er ya' took the bus – if ya' know what's good fer ya'."

With those words of wisdom imparted, he motioned for me to start closing the door. As I did so, he leaned over again, grabbing the handle, and yanked the door closed properly. I hoisted my bags out of the bed and set them on the gravel by the side of the road. I waved to the bushy bearded man as he gunned the engine and coaxed his clutch into action. By the time I had my bags on my shoulders and my guitar in hand, he was already out of sight, though I could hear him well after I'd started up the entrance ramp leading back up to I-40.

23: All the way to Memphis

This time, I did make it all the way up the ramp and had time to set up camp again. My habit was to pass the point where the lanes started to fuse, when the white line of the highway's right edge met at a point with the left line of the entrance ramp, but not go beyond that to where the entrance ramp disappeared completely. This was somehow my bargain with myself that I wasn't actually on the interstate. I fully knew that pedestrians were not technically allowed on the interstate, but this was also well before I'd ever seen one of the signs, so common these days, that specifically state something like: 'Pedestrians, non-motorized vehicles, and motor-driven cycles under 150cc prohibited beyond this point.'

So there I was, sitting technically on the side of the entrance ramp, contemplating whether to set up my stove and cook something or to eat the last of my food that didn't need to be cooked. In order to put off the decision, I pulled out my guitar and started strumming a few chords. I played two of my favorite songs from camp. I played my hitchhiking song. I might have played aimlessly for a bit. But finally a brown Pontiac pulled off the interstate, crossed the entrance ramp, and came to a stop about fifty feet up the road from me. Immediately, I saw the white reverse lights come on, and it started retreating towards me. I must admit, I did have a moment of fear that I was going to need to dive out of the way as the car plowed through my stuff, but the driver braked to a stop less than ten feet away from me.

"Y'know, Nashville's that way," the twenty-something driver greeted me as he climbed out of the car pointing back the way we'd both come. "Most of the time, the guys with guitars are headed that direction."

I just smiled and said that I'd started from there this morning with a case full of blues, but that the good people of Tennessee were helping me change my tune.

"Well if it's blues you're after, then you're headed the right direction. Memphis is the place to be!"

He helped me load my stuff into his car and we got in. As he shifted out of park and into gear he turned to me, extending his hand, "Name's Roy."

"Wade," I replied.

"Wayne?" he asked.

"No. Wade, as in the water," I answered.

"Okay, Wade. Are you headed to Memphis? 'Cause that's where I'm going. Got a girl there, and I play drums in a band. We're gonna start touring one of these days, but for now we just play in my friend's basement."

"No," I replied to the question that had been left somewhere back there, "I'm actually headed down into Mississippi. I'm eventually headed to the coast, but today I'm trying to make it to Starkville. I've got some friends that go to school there."

"Oh, well how are you going? Up a little ways in Jackson you could take US 45 south. It goes right by Starkville. But it's not a very busy road. At least I've never seen much traffic on it, except when Tennessee has a big game down there.

"Or you could go through Memphis and take I-55 down, then take 82 across to Starkville. I can get you into Memphis, easy."

I pulled out my atlas and started checking out the routes Roy was talking about. It did look like 45 was a much more direct route, but a small road in northern Mississippi also seemed more likely than the interstate to be populated by people closer in persona to the paintball guys in Connecticut, especially to someone who resembled no stereotype more closely than the quintessential dirty hippy.

"Could you swing down south of Memphis and drop me on 55 headed out of town?"

"Na, man. To get you far enough south that you

wouldn't be in danger would take way too long. Plus, I'm headed to the north side of town, anyway. That would add another hour or more to my trip. I wanna get home and see my girl."

As I was digesting all of this and trying to make a rational decision, Roy spoke up once more.

"Oh! Well there goes 45, we just passed the exit. I guess you're headed through Memphis!"

As that part of the plan seemed to decide itself, I started thinking more deeply about how to deal with Memphis. I knew I didn't want to be dropped off inside the city limits. That would make getting a ride infinitely harder, but also could make finding a place to sleep hard if it came to that. Hartford had taught me a lot about making sure to plan ahead and not get into certain situations. It was still early in the day – maybe getting on ten o'clock – so I didn't really feel like I was going to be stuck in Memphis, but I wanted some control of how to make it through safely.

I pulled out my PENN/TENN cardboard sign and checked it for a clear surface. My permanent marker had dried out somewhat, but I was able to get a good outline of MISS on it, and spent much of the drive in toward Memphis filling in the letters while also giving the pen a break. (It seemed to work better for the first few seconds after uncapping it each time.)

Roy kept rattling on about how his band was just on the edge of a big break and his girlfriend was going to go on tour with them. I was spending my time, when I was giving the pen a break, looking out the window, watching for the edge of the sprawl of Memphis. It was still early in the day, but I had to be prepared to spend the night wherever Roy dropped me off, so I didn't want it to be too deep into the outskirts of Memphis.

When we were about 30 miles from town, according to the green road signs, I asked Roy to drop me at one of the next couple of exits. He pulled off at the next one, which had the requisite number of hotels & motels, fast food joints, gas stations, and diners. It also had three nice stands of woods that I figured I could camp in if it came to that.

I bid Roy farewell, thanks, and best of luck on his music career as he drove across the intersection and directly on to the entrance ramp. As the road was clear, I followed his path, and made it across the road by the time he disappeared at the top of the ramp. It occurred to me that it would have been a better idea to ask him to drop me off up there, but it was a little too late to do anything about that now. If being kicked by the mule a second time is no longer a learning experience, then I'd been beyond learning experiences for quite some time on this trek.

On the other hand, few of my rides dropped me off and continued on their way along the interstate. There was the Magnum guy in Virginia, but that was more like the second kick from the mule of not accepting rides that make you uncomfortable. Had there been any others? Perhaps this one really was a learning experience, after all.

In any case, I made it to the top of the ramp, leaned my bags up against each other with the guitar visible out front, grabbed the MISS sign in my hands, and started putting 'pick-me-up' vibes out into the air. I waited less than fifteen minutes before the Dodge Ram pick-up pulled over, crossed the entrance ramp, and came to a stop.

24: *Memphis into Mississippi*

I quickly shouldered my bags and grabbed my guitar before trotting up to the passenger window of the truck. The man at the driver's wheel was wearing a cowboy hat, denim shirt, and blue jeans. He looked over and asked if I was headed down into Mississippi.

I told him I was headed towards Starkville and he said he could get me to highway 82, but he was headed down to Jackson. I thanked him and dropped my gear in the bed of the truck before hopping into the seat next to him.

We drove in relative silence, which gave me time to reflect on my good planning or good luck in stopping before Memphis. The drive around the city and down I-55 was uneventful for the most part. There were a couple of snippets of conversation along the way, but I dozed a little and was awakened by him as he took the exit for the junction with US 82.

There wasn't much actually at the interchange, but a sign indicated that a filling station was up the road a little ways towards Starkville. I waved goodbye to what I did not yet know was my last ride hitched from the side of the road and started east, walking on the shoulder of the highway.

As I walked from the interstate up the road to what turned out to be a huge truck stop, complete with showers and a small restaurant, I continued to think about how my appearance affected my experiences.

I think one of the best ways I ever heard it put, especially in language that your average Young White American Male would understand, is that being a white American male is like playing a video game on the easiest setting. (Not being much of a video game player myself, this is how I've played most video games I've tried.) There are a range of settings in the game of life, though – it's not just Easy, Medium, and Hard. Not living in the first world? Harder setting. Not white (or part of a country's racial or ethnic majority)? Harder setting. Not male? Harder setting. Lesbian woman of a religious minority in a third world country? One of the hardest settings, I would imagine.

I was strongly influenced in high school by a Michigan transplant to the deep south. I put it that way because Tom didn't really fit the political mold one might expect from someone living and working in the deep south. He was my boss at a furniture store and made me listen to Rush Limbaugh, because, "You've gotta know what the other side's thinking."

But he also introduced me to U. Utah Phillips, the Golden Voice of the Great Southwest. Utah Phillips is a folk singer of sorts, who also tells stories amongst his singing. He's a self-professed rabble-rouser and disruptor of the status quo. On one of his recordings, he tells the story of a discussion he had with the anarchist pacifist Ammon Hennacy:

"[Ammon] said... 'You were born a white man in mid-twentieth century industrial society. You came into the world armed to the teeth with an arsenal of weapons – the weapons of privilege: sexual privilege, racial privilege, economic privilege.... You're going to have to give up the weapons of privilege and go forth into the world completely disarmed.'

"That's hard. [It's been over] twenty years and I'm still at it. But, if there's a worthy struggle in my life, I suppose that's the one."

Twenty years after hearing that for the first time,

I'm still not exactly sure how one goes about giving up or dealing with those privileges, but I'm certainly conscious that they exist, and they make my experience on this planet different from other people who have different levels of privilege.

As I made it to the truck stop, I was grateful to find that it was cool and dark inside. I knew I was only about a half hour from Starkville, but I didn't know how long it would be until that half hour actually started. I'd already had quite a walk, so I decided there was no real hurry. I put my stuff in a corner near the pay phones and relaxed for a while.

I approached a couple of folks filling their cars at the station and asked if they might be able to give me a ride, but they all seemed pretty reluctant to even talk to me, so I gave that up relatively quickly. At one point, I tried calling my friends in Starkville, but I got their answering machine and decided not to leave a message quite yet. Some part of me wanted to get all the way there on my own instead of have someone drive way out to pick me up. Plus, it was still very early in the afternoon, and I figured I'd even give standing out on the road in the sweltering heat a shot before I threw in the towel.

It took a while, but I started watching people, especially truck drivers as they drove up. Every time a truck came from the east and stopped, they continued on to the west. The vast majority of the trucks coming from the west continued eastward, though some turned back and headed toward the interstate. It was one of those eastbound truck drivers who I approached.

I saw him stop and fill his Peterbilt rig before heading into the station. He sat at the restaurant and ate, used the facilities, and paid his bill. As he headed across the main lobby, I approached him.

25: *An 18 wheeler; my final ride*

"Excuse me, but are you headed through Starkville?"

"Yeah, why?"

"Well I'm trying to visit some friends there. I started in Maine five days ago and I've been hitchhiking across the country. I'd really appreciate a ride that way if it's not too much trouble."

"I'm headed through there now. Grab your stuff and follow me."

I hobbled after him across the blacktop and stopped outside the door of his truck. He opened it and started around the other side.

"It'll be easiest if you lift your stuff into the seat, and I'll pass it back through into the bed."

I started with the duffle bag, since it was easiest to toss around. I followed that with my backpack after I watched the trucker toss my first bag behind him. The backpack was harder for him to maneuver, so I was in the cab with the guitar before he had the backpack fully stowed. As I wedged the guitar between the other two bags, the driver spoke.

"You've been carrying all that shit from Maine? How the hell did you even get a ride carrying all that?"

"I don't really know," I replied. "Just lucky, I guess."

"Hell, if you weren't lucky, you'd be dead by now. But that's a lot of heavy shit back there. What were you doing in Maine? Mining lead?"

At which point, I started telling stories of my own. Stories of learning to play music out of necessity. Stories of friendship and trust. And maybe even a few of the stories I've shared here. Hopefully, they were enough to entertain him for the drive across

Mississippi. Hopefully, they made his choice to give me a lift worthwhile, if only to pass the time on one stretch of road.

He dropped me off at an intersection in town, and was already pulling away before I could even pick up my bags and drag them to a shady overhang. Whether it was his plan or not, I was grateful that he'd dropped me at a corner that had a pay phone, so I again dialed my friend's number. His then girlfriend, now wife, answered the phone and, after her initial shock at hearing I was in town, agreed to come over right away to pick me up and drive me to their apartment.

Somer's initial shock was nothing, however, compared to her reaction when she saw me and started coming over to say hi. To be blunt, I was a stinky mess. In spite of the late summer heat, she rolled down the windows for the drive back to their place, and was more or less insistent that the first thing I do was take a shower, which I did with no complaint. By the time I was out of the shower and dressed in some clean(er) clothes, Jimmy was home and seemed thrilled to see me. As there were still a few days before my mom's and my birthday, they agreed to let me stay with them for the intervening time and even offered to loan me one of their cars to drive down to Ocean Springs early on my birthday morning.

At this point, I started adding everything up. It had taken me five days and twenty-five rides to travel approximately 1,800 miles. I had spent $14.40 of my money, been given one ten dollar bill, and had at least three meals bought for me. I never opened my duffle bag once the entire trip. I was tired, to be sure, but no more so than any day in camp working with 9 to 14 year old boys.

All in all, it was an experience that has stuck with

me throughout my life, given me (hopefully) interesting stories and vignettes to tell, and made me more self-reliant than any other single experience in my lifetime. And best of all, I was never threatened, injured, abducted, abused, or robbed.

Day 6: Starkville to Ocean Springs

or

"What do you mean you're not happy to see me, Mom?"

On the morning of our birthday, I got up ridiculously early. I knew my mom was an early riser, and I figured she had plans of some sort for that day, so I wanted to arrive before 7:00 AM, if I possibly could, so I must have left Starkville around two in the morning. As I recall, I drove into her driveway around 6:50, and she happened to see me through the window. She was out of the house and walking up to me before I could even get out of the car.

Her initial thrill at seeing me quickly gave way to

the incredulous question of how I got there. In hindsight, it was a mistake to be completely honest right from the start. I could have easily dodged the question by saying that I'd been planning this since camp ended, that I was excited to see her for our birthday, that I wanted to share my twentieth birthday with her, or any number of other options.

Instead, I heard myself answer the specific question that had been asked.

"I hitchhiked."

It kind of burst the whole happy birthday bubble and made the next couple of hours somewhat tense, to say the least. I mean, I could offer many points of advice about things to do and things not to do while hitchhiking, but, if this book has any major take-away, it should be this: if you hitchhike across the country to surprise your mom for her birthday (or any other occasion), DO NOT TELL HER THAT YOU HITCHHIKED. At least not right away. Or even that day. Possibly for at least a year afterwards. Or ever.

My warm reception turned quickly into a chilly lecture, or at least a series of cold looks. Somehow I'd turned my warm-fuzzy into a cold-prickly with no effort whatsoever. But, like all the other aspects of this story, it's another life lesson to be learned.

There are quite a few life lessons inherent in these pages, though I think some of them, specifically those that relate to hitchhiking, could bear repeating.

Don't accept rides that don't feel right.

Don't get into the middle seat.

Don't get into a car with someone who has to move condoms to let you sit down.

Don't carry too much crap.

Don't turn down a warm dry place to stay the night (assuming you get good vibes from the person offering).

And, most importantly:

Don't tell your mom you've been hitchhiking.

I also have a series of positive suggestions, though they have to follow the caveat that hitchhiking is inherently dangerous and you should reconsider your travel plans if they include hitchhiking. If, after deeply thinking about paintball gunners, condom-laden pick-ups, and other sorts of nefarious ne'er-do-wells, you still think that hitchhiking is a good idea, call your mom and talk to her about it. If you cannot be dissuaded, here are some other tips.

Have a sign that states a destination not too far away. Bonus points if you can change the sign along the way.

Carry a guitar (or other highly visible musical instrument) that you know how to play. It's good both for getting rides and not caring as much if you don't get rides.

Have a credit card or a prepaid card so you can get yourself out of potentially dangerous situations, whether that's a motel room to not freeze at night, a bus ticket out of a city at night, or a meal when you really need one.

And, above all else,

Follow your gut. Somehow, it knows more than you do.

Epilogue

For about a decade after my trip, I made every effort to pick up hitchhikers, though I did always give my passengers (who were already in the car with me) veto options if they weren't comfortable with the idea. Seeing the experience from that side has been educational as well.

There are truisms. Hitchhikers tend to stink. Offering them a ride doesn't automatically ensure gratitude. They come in the talkative and semi-mute varieties that I also experienced with those who gave me rides. But they all have stories to tell, experiences to share, and, whether physical or metaphorical, destinations to which they are headed.

I do admit that I have raised my standards about what sorts of people I'll invite in to my car, and I do now have times that I'm not willing to stop for someone. If a person is not putting any effort into getting a ride – such as the guy I saw asleep on an on-ramp, lying on top of his bags; or someone just walking down the interstate – I'm unlikely to stop. Someone has to at least ask me. It doesn't take that much effort to stick out a thumb or hold up a sign telling where you're going.

And I'm incredibly unlikely to stop for someone if my family is in the car with me. There are just too many stories out there for me to risk my family's safety, but I don't believe that the vast majority of hitchhikers, even today, have dastardly designs. But still, the same advice goes for picking up a hitchhiker that was offered for accepting a ride. If it doesn't feel right, don't do it.

Which is why I am not offended when I have been turned down by hitchhikers. Well, to be completely honest, that's only happened once. I was lost in thought headed along the interstate when I saw someone hitchhiking out of the corner of my eye. I was already passing them, but I slammed on the brakes (squealing more than just a little, if memory serves), pulled over to the shoulder, then backed up to the person.

She turned out to be a highly attractive young woman who I had just given the heebie-jeebies to. As she turned me down, I was momentarily confused, but quickly realized that, had I been waiting for a ride and someone had pulled over the way I had just done so, it's unlikely I would have gotten in their car either. So I wished her the best of luck and continued on my way.

The final words with which I will leave the reader concern the reason it has taken me almost two decades to put these stories on paper and submit them, hopefully, for your enjoyment. We all know the stories of the hitchhiker who gets abducted or the friendly young couple who gets carjacked. Reading my stories may inspire someone – it is always my hope as a writer to inspire my reader – to take to the open road. In this case, however, I cannot advocate that anyone follow any of the ideas, advice, or hair-brained plans offered within these pages. The world is not an ideal place, and the bad guys are out there. I don't want to be responsible for someone going off and getting themselves into trouble. I wish this book to be read with an occasional chuckle as the reader contemplates the poor judgment of a young man rather than a call to (mis)adventure.

Remember, anyone who does attempt to hitchhike is taking huge risks on multiple levels. You truly are on your own out there, without a safety net. I wouldn't try this. (Oh wait, I did.) I can't believe I did this. I do have to offer my sincere apologies to any family or friends who had bad things happen to them that week back in September of 1993. I must have had guardian angels sending out for reinforcements from anyone even remotely connected to me. That I made it through these experiences not only alive and well, but reasonably unscarred, both emotionally and physically, is a testament to those whose love and energy, and yes, angels, surrounded me, protected me, and sustained me. Thank you.

ABOUT THE AUTHOR

Wade C. Davis is an author, educator, parent, gardener, and musician who lives in Ann Arbor, Michigan, with his family. This is his second book, and will likely be his only memoir.

Wade doffs his hat to Justin and the crew that successfully moved The Bug to the Concert Hall several years later. And to Kareem, who hid in a garbage can for three hours, prepared to let us in to the student union.

All maps pictured in this book were taken from GoogleMaps.

Front Cover Photo © 2006 Wade C Davis

Back Cover Author Photo © 2007 Cathy L Foster
Find Cathy's photography online at
http://www.cathyfosterphotography.com

Made in the USA
Monee, IL
06 October 2021